Dinosaurs and People

BY THE SAME AUTHOR

DINOSAURS AND THEIR WORLD

THE CONTROVERSIAL COYOTE:
Predation, Politics, and Ecology

LAURENCE PRINGLE

Dinosaurs and People

FOSSILS, FACTS, and FANTASIES

ILLUSTRATED WITH PHOTOGRAPHS
AND DRAWINGS

Harcourt Brace Jovanovich

New York and London

Requests for permission to make copies of any part of the work should be mailed to: Permissions, Harcourt Brace Jovanovich, Inc., 757 Third Avenue, New York, N.Y. 10017

Printed in the United States of America

Library of Congress Cataloging in Publication Data

Pringle, Laurence P

    Dinosaurs and people.

    Bibliography: p.

    Includes index.

    SUMMARY: Traces the research on dinosaurs since the first discoveries of their fossils and presents some of the startling new ideas now being considered regarding what they were really like.

    1. Dinosauria—Juvenile literature. 2. Paleontology —History—Juvenile literature. [1. Dinosaurs. 2. Paleontology—History] I. Title.

QE862.D5P73   568'.19   78-52810

ISBN 0-15-260501-0

First edition

B C D E

The author wishes to thank Dr. John H. Ostrom, Professor of Geology, Division of Vertebrate Paleontology, Peabody Museum of Natural History, Yale University, for reading and suggesting changes in the manuscript of this book.

CONTENTS

U. S. 2038173

From the author's snowy New York yard to a sunny California playground,
dinosaurs are alive in our imaginations.

1

UNKNOWN, UNNAMED CREATURES

Dinosaur is a magic word. Soon after children learn to say their own names, they proudly pronounce the names of some dinosaurs: *Stegosaurus, Brontosaurus,* and especially *Tyrannosaurus rex.*

Long after childhood, people are still fascinated by the word dinosaur. There is nothing make-believe about these creatures. Dinosaurs really existed, and some of them resembled terrifying dragons or monsters.

People like to be frightened, at least a little bit. They also like the idea that there are still mysteries around. Life might be boring if we understood everything about nature and about ourselves. Knowing what we do about dinosaurs, and wondering about them, adds spice to our lives.

For a few people, a fascination with dinosaurs includes the hope that they may still exist on other planets or even on earth. These people dream that somewhere there may be an undiscovered island in the tropics, or a hidden valley in the jungle that has been cut off from the rest of the world for millions of years. Someday it will be

"Live" dinosaurs—in this case, a greatly enlarged lizard—
have appeared in more than a dozen films.

found. Then explorers will venture into this wild place
and, suddenly, live dinosaurs will appear!

Fantasies like this have been made into movies,
novels, and television shows. Such fantasies are fun, but,
alas, they are just wishful thinking. The world is well
explored by now, and scientists do not expect to find any
living dinosaurs.

Newspaper comic strips and television cartoons show
cavemen and cavewomen living with dinosaurs. This is
fantasy too. The dinosaurs died out long before humans
lived on earth. There is no doubt, however, that dinosaurs
did once exist. They were the main form of life on land for

more than 140 million years, while humans have been living on earth for only about four million years. That is reason enough to find them fascinating. As new facts and ideas continue to appear, our understanding of dinosaurs grows and changes. This is exciting too.

Almost everything we know about these remarkable animals we have learned from fossils—bones, teeth, whole skeletons, body imprints, tracks, and other signs of past life that have been preserved in rocks. Early humans probably noticed fossils and wondered about them. Indians in the American West feared the big fossil skeletons they found. They believed that the fossils were the remains of serpents that the Great Spirit had killed with lightning bolts.

Europeans also found fossil bones of dinosaurs and other extinct animals, such as mammoths. Like the Indians, their imaginations ran wild about these strange objects. Big fossil bones were thought to be the remains of giant people or of dragons. Some people believed that fossils were parts of "models" that God had discarded before creating life, or that perhaps they were creatures that had been too big to fit into Noah's ark and had drowned.

In 1802 a Massachusetts farm boy found some large footprints in a rock quarry. The prints showed three pointed toes. They looked like bird tracks. People assumed that the footprints were made by ancient birds, which they called "Noah's ravens."

A minister and professor named Edward B. Hitchcock spent many years collecting fossil footprints in New England. He published a book about them and speculated

Looking at fossil footprints of "Noah's ravens"—dinosaurs

about the lives of these "peculiar and gigantic" birds. We now know that the footprints were made by dinosaurs.

Edward Hitchcock is a good example of the sort of person who studied fossils in the early 1800s. At that time very few people went to college. Those who did were almost always men, and many of them were trained to be ministers or medical doctors. The doctors were taught human anatomy—how a person's bones, muscles, and organs are arranged. They also studied the anatomy of other animals.

Some doctors and other educated men were especially interested in nature, animal bones, and fossils. In addition to their regular work, they searched for fossils and studied them. The curiosity of these men led to the discovery of dinosaurs.

One such man was Gideon Mantell, a doctor who was born and raised in southern England. As a boy Mantell played in the countryside around his hometown. He saw fossils in local stone quarries and was fascinated by them. Later when, as a doctor, he made house calls in the country, he collected fossils along the roadsides and tried to identify them. Most were sea shells. In 1822 Mantell published a book called *The Fossils of the South Downs*. It was illustrated with many drawings by his wife, Mary.

Mary Mantell sometimes accompanied her husband on his rounds. One spring day in 1822, while waiting outdoors as the doctor visited a patient, she noticed a strange-looking rock by the road. She picked it up and saw fossil teeth in the rock. The Mantells were excited by this discovery, but neither of them could imagine how these few teeth would affect the rest of their lives.

Gideon Mantell searched for more fossils in that area. He also asked for help from workers in stone quarries. More teeth, and fossil bones as well, were found. From the shape of the teeth Mantell concluded that they were from a plant-eating animal. But what kind of animal?

He showed the fossil teeth and bones to other men who studied fossils. Mantell was told that the fossils were from a large fish or a large mammal, such as a rhinoceros or hippopotamus. He was also told that the fossils might not be very old. They may have been accidentally washed by water in among some very old rocks but were really from more recent times.

These opinions disappointed Mantell. He believed that he had discovered the remains of an ancient animal, perhaps a reptile, so he kept on with his investigations. He traveled to London and visited the Royal College of Surgeons. In a museum there he examined the bones and teeth of different kinds of reptiles, including snakes, crocodiles, and lizards. None looked like his fossils. Then, purely by chance, he met a young man named Samuel Stutchbury at the museum.

Stutchbury was interested in iguanas, large lizards that live in Central and South America. He showed an iguana to Mantell, who immediately saw that the unidentified fossil teeth were like iguana teeth, only much bigger. He soon published an important scientific article about his discovery, calling the ancient reptile *Iguanodon*

Mary Mantell made detailed drawings of the Iguanodon teeth and vertebrae that her husband found.

(which means "iguana tooth"). In this way the idea of big ancient reptiles was born.

Gideon Mantell won fame as the discoverer of Iguanodon. But there must have been times when his wife wished that she had never showed him those old teeth by the road. The study of fossils became an obsession with Mantell.

After moving to a larger town, he turned his new home into a sort of museum. Fossils were stored or displayed in almost every room. Mantell neglected his medical work and ran short of money. He had to sell his precious fossils to a science museum, but his obsession continued. Fossils came first, and he neglected his family. Eventually his wife and children left him.

The story of dinosaurs and people is therefore not only one of exciting discoveries and fame; for the Mantells it was also one of hardship and heartbreak.

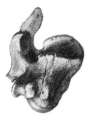

2

PIONEERS IN PALEONTOLOGY

The actual name, dinosaur, was coined in 1841 by Richard Owen. Like Mantell, he had been trained as a doctor. His main interest, however, was comparing the anatomy of one kind of animal with that of other kinds. Eventually, Richard Owen became a leading British scientist.

Fascinated by the discoveries of Mantell and others, Owen himself studied and described some extinct animals. From his investigations he concluded that "these bones represented reptiles belonging to a large group that had long since vanished from the earth."

For this group of animals he proposed the name *Dinosauria* (from Greek words meaning "terrible lizard"). Actually giving a name to these ancient creatures was an important step. It helped catch the interest of many people, especially men who were pioneers in the science of paleontology—the study of the earth's ancient life.

More fossils were found in England, including more parts of Iguanodon skeletons. These discoveries were particularly useful to men like Richard Owen. To an

An unusual New Year's Eve party ➤

anatomist, the shapes of bones can reveal a lot about the animal they once supported. From a nearly complete skeleton it is possible to get an idea of an animal's shape, size, and weight. It is also possible to figure out whether the animal walked on two legs or four, how fast it may have moved, and other facts about its life.

In the mid-1800s, of course, this kind of research was quite new. A lot of it was guesswork, and there were few fossil bones to study. Nevertheless, the idea of exploring past life in this way appealed to Richard Owen. With the aid of a sculptor named Benjamin Waterhouse Hawkins, he set out to make three-dimensional, life-size models of some extinct animals, including Iguanodon. For materials they used iron, bricks, tiles, stones, and concrete.

The reconstructions were made in the 1850s and can still be seen in a London park. A famous dinner party was held on New Year's Eve, 1853, *inside* a half-finished Iguanodon. Richard Owen sat at the head of the table, which was, naturally, at the head of the dinosaur!

When completed, the Iguanodon reconstructions looked somewhat like huge rhinoceroses. About 35 feet long, they stood on four short, thick legs. On the snout of each dinosaur was a spike, like the horn of a rhino.

Many years passed before this picture of Iguanodon changed. Eventually, many Iguanodon fossils, including complete skeletons, were discovered. Paleontologists had more evidence to study and had also learned more about reconstructing extinct animals. Today we have a very different view of this dinosaur. It walked on strong hind legs, standing upright, perhaps somewhat like a kangaroo. And it had spikes on each thumb, not on its nose.

We can chuckle about the misplaced spikes on Owen's Iguanodons, but he was a pioneer working with very little information. There is no doubt, however, about

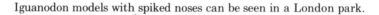

Iguanodon models with spiked noses can be seen in a London park.

the importance of his studies. They helped spread the news about dinosaurs all over the world.

More remains of dinosaurs were found and identified in Europe and North America. In 1858, a scientist published news of an almost-complete dinosaur skeleton that had been dug up in the state of New Jersey. Called *Hadrosaurus,* it was one of the duck-billed dinosaurs that were once so abundant in North America.

In 1868 an ambitious attempt was made to reconstruct life-size models of Hadrosaurus and other ancient creatures. There was to be a grand museum in Central Park in New York City. The man who built those Iguanodons in London—Benjamin Waterhouse Hawkins— was hired to re-create American prehistoric life.

Iguanodons are now known to have had spikes on their forelimbs.

Hawkins traveled to science museums and studied the remains of Hadrosaurus and other fossils. A workshop was set up in Central Park. The foundations for the museum itself were laid. Hawkins and his assistants worked on reconstructions of several creatures, including two models of Hadrosaurus, one 39 feet long. Then, after two years of work, disaster struck—not from fire or earthquake, but from politics.

A group of corrupt politicians called the Tweed Ring had taken control of the city government. They grew rich from shady deals and robbing the public treasury. They saw no profit in making a display of ancient animals. Funds for the museum were cut off and the foundations filled in. But Benjamin Waterhouse Hawkins kept working on his models. He hoped that they might be bought by a science museum in another city.

For some reason the Tweed Ring decided to prevent even this. In the spring of 1871, hired vandals raided Hawkins's workshop. The dinosaur models were smashed with sledgehammers and the remains taken away and buried. Smaller models and Hawkins's sketches were also destroyed. A Tweed Ring politician advised Hawkins that he "should not bother himself about dead animals, when there were so many living ones to care for."

Hawkins fled New York City. Before long the Tweed Ring itself was smashed, but plans for a dinosaur display in Central Park were not revived. Hawkins later painted imaginary scenes of dinosaurs and their surroundings, but his dreams of creating a whole museum of ancient life were shattered along with his models.

Hawkins had good reason to feel bitter and disap-

PALAEOZOIC MUSEUM.
SHOWING THE REHABILITATED FORMS OF ANCIENT ANIMAL LIFE IN AMERICA.
NOW BEING CONSTRUCTED IN CENTRAL PARK.

A view of the proposed Central Park museum, victim of Tweed Ring politics in New York City

pointed. However, the fact that some people in New York City had tried to build this museum showed that there was a strong interest in "dead animals." Despite the Tweed Ring, the story of dinosaurs and people had reached an exciting new stage of interest, exploration, and discovery.

3

THE GREAT DINOSAUR RUSH

In the 1870s and 1880s many people became interested in the past life of North America. Paleontology was no longer a sort of hobby for medical doctors; it was a respected and important science. Museums and universities wanted to have fossils to study. Some rich men were eager to spend money to achieve this goal. Railroads reached far into the West, where the discovery of many fossils was reported. The stage was set for a sort of western dinosaur "rush," like the gold rushes of California and Colorado.

For many years two men dominated this dinosaur rush. They were Othniel Marsh and Edward Cope. In some ways they were like Gideon Mantell and others who had preceded them. As boys, both Cope and Marsh were interested in the outdoors, nature, and fossils. But they later had the advantage of scientific training, which enabled them to become leaders in the rapidly growing field of paleontology. They also had the advantage of family wealth.

Early in their careers, Marsh visited Cope for a week.

They reportedly had a pleasant time looking for fossils in New Jersey, but both knew more about competing than about cooperating. Before long they became bitter rivals. Marsh and Cope were to fight for the rest of their lives for scientific prestige and success. In their battle the weapons were collections of fossils and their writings about them.

One of the most extraordinary fossil-hunting places in the West was Como Bluff in Wyoming. The bluff was a long ridge that stretched along the Union Pacific Railroad tracks. Two railroad workers wrote to Othniel Marsh about "gigantic bones" they had found there. He soon hired these men and others to dig out the fossils. And dig they did, in all seasons including winter, when temperatures fell far below zero. The men sometimes had to remove drifted snow from the fossils before they could work on them.

When collected, a fossil bone is often removed while still enclosed in the original rock or soil surrounding it. Removal of the enclosing rock may take many hours of painstaking work; it can be done best later, in the laboratory. Also, the bone may be brittle and break into small bits as it is worked on. Therefore, in order to prevent this and to save time, a fossil is often only partly exposed. Then it and some surrounding rock are covered with a coating of plaster. This protects the fossil in the same way a plaster cast protects a broken arm or leg. Usually fossils are further protected by being packed in wooden crates.

Trains from Como Bluff carried tons of fossil packages east to Othniel Marsh. News of the discoveries spread quickly. Within a few months, a fossil-hunting crew hired by Edward Cope was also at Como Bluff.

Western North America yielded fossils of many kinds of dinosaurs.

Marsh's men did their best to keep Cope's workers away from the richest fossil grounds.

Some historians say that the men once battled with fists, but others say that the only clashes occurred back east as Cope and Marsh examined fossils and wrote articles about them for scientific journals. In their haste to be "first," they sometimes made mistakes. And, of course, each took great pleasure in pointing out the other's errors.

The competition between these men had some good effects. Their work crews unearthed many tons of fossils. These included not just dinosaurs but also the remains of other kinds of extinct animals and plants.

News of these discoveries increased national interest in paleontology. The federal government gave some funds—mostly to Marsh—for fossil-hunting. People all over the country became more dinosaur conscious. Of course this sometimes caused them to get all excited when they found an old cow bone in a pasture, but at other times valuable fossils were found accidentally.

In 1887, some geologists found a pair of fossil horns near Denver. They sent the horns to Marsh, who decided that they were from an extinct kind of bison (buffalo). However, a year later some Montana cowboys found similar horns, which were attached to a complete skull.

Marsh changed his mind about this horned animal. He had the first remains of *Triceratops* ("three-horned face"). Eventually, hundreds of such skulls and other body parts were found in the West. Triceratops and its relatives looked somewhat like rhinoceroses, and great herds of these horned dinosaurs once grazed on plants in North America and eastern Asia.

Marsh and his collectors also discovered the first specimen of the huge *Brontosaurus* ("thunder lizard"). Most of his fossils are now in either the Peabody Museum of Natural History at Yale University or the National Museum in Washington, D.C. Most of Cope's collection is at the American Museum of Natural History in New York City.

Partly because of their feud, Cope and Marsh received most of the attention and fame during the dinosaur "rush" days. However, other men, including some of their former helpers, also had remarkable dinosaur-hunting careers.

John Bell Hatcher, for example, collected fossils for Marsh and later for universities and science museums. He was a good geologist and an even better poker player. Money he won from poker games helped pay for his fossil-hunting trips to western North America and South America.

Another successful dinosaur-hunter was Charles Sternberg. As a young boy he collected fossil sea shells. As a teen-ager he collected fossil leaves in Kansas. "At the age of seventeen," he later wrote, "I made up my mind what part I should play in life. . . . I would make it my business to collect facts from the crust of the earth."

In the spring of 1876, Charles Sternberg tried to join an expedition that was setting out for western Kansas to collect fossils for Marsh. All of the jobs were filled, but Sternberg didn't give up. He wrote directly to Edward Cope, told him of his eagerness to hunt for fossils, and asked for $300.

In those days that sum of money was enough to buy a wagon, a team of horses, food and other supplies, and the services of a driver and a cook for the entire summer. Cope, impressed by Sternberg's letter, sent the money by return mail, and Charles Sternberg was launched on a fossil-hunting career that would last nearly seventy years—until he died at the age of ninety-three.

During that time Sternberg collected fossils for both Cope and Marsh, and also for the Geological Survey of Canada. He was often helped by his three sons, each of whom later took up fossil-collecting and paleontology as a career. During the early 1900s they all sought dinosaurs near the Red Deer River in the province of Alberta,

Among the dinosaurs discovered in western North America were Triceratops *(top left)*, an ostrich dinosaur, and Brontosaurus (whose official name is Apatosaurus).

Dinosaur skeletons uncovered in Utah, at Dinosaur National Monument

Canada. Other fossil-hunters explored this area too. Among the discoveries were several kinds of duck-billed dinosaurs and the meat-eating *Gorgosaurus.*

Charles Sternberg and his sons had many adventures and successes in their work, but there were disappointments and dangers too. One time, walking across steep, smooth rock in Montana, Sternberg lost his footing, slid downhill, and stopped just before falling over a thousand-foot cliff. Another time Sternberg and one of his sons had carefully unearthed a seven-foot-long skull of Triceratops, only to have it destroyed by a tornado.

In 1916 Sternberg and his youngest son, Levi, collected some dinosaurs in Canada for the British Museum. The best finds that summer were two skeletons of duck-billed dinosaurs. They were packed up and put aboard a steamship that was bound for Britain. The dinosaurs never arrived, however, because a German submarine torpedoed the ship and sent it and its cargo to the bottom of the Atlantic.

When we read about the Sternbergs or other fossil collectors, we tend to think only of the exciting times—of discovering a new kind of dinosaur or some other important fossil. We tend to forget the hardships. The day-to-day routine of dinosaur-hunting was just plain hard work. It continued regardless of the weather—mud or dust, cold or hot. The men were familiar with the sounds of howling winds, whining mosquitoes, and buzzing rattlesnakes. Sometimes very few fossils were found, food supplies ran short, and the morale of the workers sank low.

This was the case in 1908, when the four Sternbergs were working in southern Wyoming. Two of the brothers stayed near camp while the other two men drove a wagon to the nearest town, sixty miles away, for some badly needed supplies.

The only food left in camp was potatoes. So the Sternbergs ate potatoes, dreamed of other kinds of food, and kept looking for fossils. It was at this low point that they made an extraordinary discovery—the first specimen of dinosaur *skin!* It wasn't edible, but the Sternbergs didn't care. This discovery of a duck-billed dinosaur with the fine details of its skin preserved in stone is one of the most unusual finds in the history of paleontology.

The great North American dinosaur rush ended in the early 1900s. By then, science museums in the United States and Canada had large collections of dinosaur fossils. Now they faced the task of separating fossils from rocks, cleaning them, protecting them, storing them, and also studying them. All this took money and time. In one case, a big dinosaur shoulder blade had broken into 80 pieces. The job of cleaning the parts, putting them back together, and strengthening the bone took 160 hours.

There was enough work to keep paleontologists and their helpers busy indoors for many years.

4

TENDAGURU, GOBI, AND WOMEN, TOO

Although paleontologists had plenty of North American dinosaur fossils to study, they wondered what might be found on other continents. About the time the dinosaur rush was ending in North America, German scientists made some exciting discoveries in East Africa.

In what is now Tanzania, a German explorer found a dinosaur "graveyard." Huge bones lay in the tall grass, gleaming in the sun. He reported his discovery to the Berlin Museum. Money was raised, and one of the greatest of all dinosaur-hunting expeditions was launched in 1909—to a place called Tendaguru.

As many as 500 men were hired as diggers or carriers of fossils. There was no railroad or highway near the fossil "digs." Every bone had to be carried overland on the backs or heads of laborers, who hiked four days to the nearest seaport. In four years more than 200 tons of dinosaur bones were moved in this way.

Among the discoveries were African relatives of Stegosaurus, and a skeleton of *Brachiosaurus,* a huge dinosaur related to Brontosaurus. In later years Tendaguru also yielded dinosaurs to a British expedition. In all, so many fossils have been found at Tendaguru that the name is as famous among paleontologists as Como Bluff and the Red Deer River.

As scientists learned more about the earth's past, they were better able to tell the age of rock layers and to judge whether they might find fossils in them. In the 1920s, however, there was one huge area about which very little was known. This was central Asia and especially the vast desert known as the Gobi, which lies mostly in Mongolia.

The enthusiasm and persistence of one man—Roy Chapman Andrews—helped persuade others that an expedition to Mongolia was worthwhile. It was sponsored by the American Museum of Natural History and led by Andrews, who was a scientist at the museum.

One excavation at Tendaguru exposed the skeleton of a huge Brachiosaurus.

The first expedition, in 1922, went so well that others followed. In all there were five, during five springs and summers. In some ways they were very modern explorations. Automobiles were used, which carried scientists far and fast over the barren Gobi. However, the expeditions were basically dependent on a caravan of 125 camels used not only to carry gasoline for the cars and food and other supplies, but also to haul out the dinosaur bones that the expedition had found.

Among the fossil treasures were primitive horned dinosaurs. They were called *Protoceratops* ("first horned face"). The fossils included skulls and skeletons of both adults and young—and, most remarkable of all, *eggs*. Some of the eggs were found preserved in a neat circle, just as a mother Protoceratops had left them, perhaps 90 million years before.

The early success of these expeditions was fortunate because the Gobi soon became a difficult and dangerous place to seek fossils. Wars and political turmoil brought an end to exploration there, but paleontologists kept in mind that someday, in more peaceful times, the Gobi would be a good place to explore further.

In the late 1940s, expeditions from the Soviet Union brought paleontologists back to the Gobi. They found more Protoceratops and eggs. They also discovered rich fossil deposits in the Nemegetu Basin of Mongolia. One place there had so many dinosaur bones they called it "The Dragon's Tomb."

Trucks carried 120 tons of fossils in their protective plaster and crates out of the Gobi. Among them were *tarbosaurs*—dinosaurs very much like the meat-eating

From Tendaguru, Africans carried 200 tons of dinosaur fossils about 40 miles
to the nearest seaport, while camels and cars *(below)* were used on early Gobi expeditions.

Tyrannosaurus of North America. Soviet scientists also found skeletons of a kind of duck-billed dinosaur *(Saurolophus),* which had been also found in North America. These discoveries supported the idea that Asia and North America had once been connected and thus had similar kinds of dinosaurs and other life.

Some skeletons from Mongolia were reconstructed and are now displayed in Soviet museums. During the early 1960s, Polish and Mongolian scientists made plans to further explore the Gobi. The expeditions were to be led by a woman.

Until recently, the story of dinosaurs and people had been mostly a story of dinosaurs and men. For a long time, studies of fossils and paleontology and especially rugged expeditions were considered "men's work." At most, women were allowed to be helpers and assistants. They made drawings (as Mary Mantell did) or worked on fossils in laboratories. Fortunately, these ideas have changed, in paleontology as well as in many other fields. The story of dinosaurs and people now includes women.

A nearly complete skeleton of a tarbosaur, an Asian dinosaur related to Tyrannosaurus.

In 1961, for example, a young Norwegian geologist named Natascha Heintz was one of four scientists who made a brief but important visit to Spitzbergen, an island in the Arctic. She and the other scientists made plaster casts of some big dinosaur tracks that had been discovered in a rock cliff, right by the sea. The tracks were later identified as those of Iguanodon—the big plant-eating dinosaur named by Gideon Mantell.

At about the same time, scientists from Poland and Mongolia agreed to cooperate on an expedition to the Gobi. A paleontologist named Zofia Kielan-Jaworowska was chosen as leader. As a paleontology student she had been fascinated by stories of the American expeditions to the Gobi. Later she followed reports of the Soviet explorers with great interest. To collect fossils in the Gobi herself was like a dream come true.

These expeditions, like the ones before, were aimed at finding all sorts of fossils. The basic goal of paleontology is to trace the history of life on earth. Just as important as the remains of dinosaurs are the tiny bones and teeth of little mammals that lived with the dinosaurs.

After a brief exploratory trip in 1963, the Polish and Mongolian scientists spent several summers in the Gobi. They traveled by truck and camped in tents. The crew of about twenty included several women besides Zofia Kielan-Jaworowska. They all endured long days of hard work in the desert sun.

Water was scarce, but a lot was needed, not just for drinking and washing but for mixing plaster to protect fossils. Often the nearest supply of water was twenty miles away from the work area. One June the crew made camp right near a well. Unfortunately, this was also the season and place for clouds of tiny, biting flies to breed. The crew was forced to move a safe distance from the well.

Sometimes their camps were struck by sandstorms, which blew down tents, ripped the canvas, and scattered wooden boards and other objects far and wide.

These hardships seemed worthwhile, however, considering the discoveries made. Two skeletons of "ostrich" dinosaurs were found—the first evidence that this group of dinosaurs lived in Asia. The crew also unearthed the skeleton of a huge *sauropod*—a dinosaur related to Brontosaurus and Brachiosaurus.

In 1965 Zofia Kielan-Jaworowska herself made a sensational discovery. Exploring alone, she saw some large foot bones sticking out of a little hill. Clearing away

Geologist Natascha Heintz *(second from right)* collected casts of Iguanodon tracks found about 700 miles from the North Pole.

The Polish-Mongolian expeditions endured fierce sandstorms in the Gobi. The leader of these highly successful fossil-hunts was Zofia Kielan-Jaworowska *(far right)*.▶

some sand, she uncovered a claw which measured 12 inches along its curved length. No known dinosaur had such big claws.

In the days that followed, she and others carefully removed sand from the remains of this unidentified dinosaur. They found most of the bones of this animal's shoulders, the two front legs, and both hands. Except for

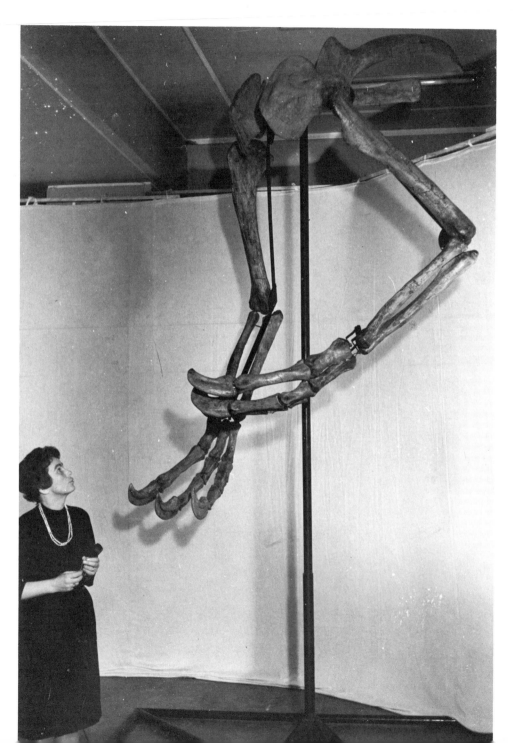

parts of a few ribs, nothing else of the dinosaur remained. There was no skull.

Nevertheless, the bones they had collected revealed quite a lot about the dinosaur and its importance. It seemed to be related to big meat-eating dinosaurs, such as the well-known Tyrannosaurus rex. But Tyrannosaurus rex had small front legs, just 30 inches long, which were of little use for food-getting. It probably killed its prey with its powerful hind legs and its sharp teeth. Its name means "king of the tyrant lizards," and many people think of Tyrannosaurus rex as the terror of the dinosaur world.

However, the dinosaur found by Zofia Kielan-Jaworowska appears to have been a big meat-eater. Unlike Tyrannosaurus rex, it had powerful front legs, 8½ feet long, tipped with big, sharp claws. This dinosaur, named *Deinocheirus,* may have been more of a "king" than Tyrannosaurus rex, but without the skull, or at least its teeth, we can't be sure.

Professor Kielan-Jaworowska looks at the reconstructed forelimbs of Deinocheirus, the extraordinary dinosaur she found.

5

THE DASHING DINOSAURS

During the middle of this century, there was a kind of lull in the story of dinosaurs and people. Except for continued interest in the Gobi, there were no major dinosaur-hunting expeditions. Most paleontologists devoted their attention to creatures such as early mammals—the ancestors of today's horses, dogs, and humans. Dinosaurs, after all, were thought to be a dead end.

Certain kinds of dinosaurs, however, became household words because they were the ones displayed in museums and illustrated in dozens of children's books. As children grew up and became adults, they found the same names and information repeated in the books of *their* children: "Stegosaurus," "Brontosaurus," and especially "Tyrannosaurus rex."

So far as the general public was concerned, the world of dinosaurs was fascinating but held few surprises. This lull was deceptive. It was one of those calm periods before a storm—in this case, a storm of new ideas.

Even though there were no headline-making expeditions, some paleontologists still studied dinosaurs and

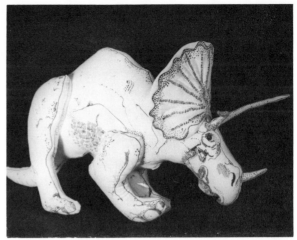

It is fun to hunt for signs of long-dead dinosaurs in our everyday lives, for example, in stuffed toys (designed by Michelle Lipson) and Polish postage stamps. On the following pages are further discoveries of this modern dinosaur hunt.

For more than forty years a brontosaur was a trademark of the Sinclair Oil Corporation, now extinct. A similar sauropod, called Dino, was one of the most popular floats used in Macy's Thanksgiving Day Parade in New York City *(next page, far right)*. Though dinosaurs and humans never lived together, they are often shown that way: on a pinball machine *(below)* and in an Arizona miniature golf course *(next page, top left)* and in Alley Oop, newspaper comic strip *(next page, bottom)*.

EEEYAHOOOOooo!

A modern dinosaur-hunting expedition will find them on television and even along highways.

kept searching for dinosaur fossils. The expeditions were small-scale but important. The goal was not to dig up yet another horned dinosaur but to look for unknown creatures or "missing links" in the chain of dinosaur development. One such discovery was made in Colorado, where, in 1972, bones of a huge sauropod were found. Its shoulder blades were eight feet long. This dinosaur, unofficially called Supersaurus, may have weighed a hundred tons, and may have been the largest land animal of all time.

Also, old collections of fossils were re-examined or examined carefully for the first time. (For example, one unusual dinosaur, collected in 1914, was not thoroughly studied and described until 1969.)

However, what was even more important was that paleontologists had much more information about past and present life. In a sense, they could look at fossils and other clues with new and much sharper eyesight. As they did this, some paleontologists began to question old ideas about dinosaurs, including some of the most basic "facts."

Nothing about dinosaurs is more basic than the idea that they were reptiles. In fact, the Mesozoic Era, all 160 million years of it, is called the Age of Reptiles because reptiles in general and dinosaurs in particular were the dominant form of life in that period.

The skeletons of dinosaurs in some ways resemble lizards, crocodiles, and other living reptiles. So Richard Owen, Edward Cope, Othniel Marsh, and many other paleontologists assumed that dinosaurs were much like living reptiles in other ways too. They assumed that dinosaurs were "cold blooded," as living reptiles are.

The term "cold blooded" is common but confusing. The blood of lizards and other reptiles is usually no cooler than yours. It may even be warmer. But reptiles warm their blood and their entire bodies in a different way than humans do. They get most of their heat from *outside* their bodies, especially by lying in the sun. Rather than "cold blooded," a better name is ectothermic, which means "getting heat from outside." (This term is easy to remember if you just recall that "ecto" means outside.)

Birds and mammals, including humans, have been called "warm blooded." Again, this term is misleading. The key characteristic is not the temperature of the blood but the way in which animals get and maintain their body heat. Birds and mammals do this mostly by burning food energy *inside* their bodies. They are endothermic, a term that means "getting heat from inside." ("Endo" means inside.)

Since dinosaurs were believed to be reptiles, they were thought to be ectothermic. If we judge from today's reptiles, what does this tell us about their lives?

It means that dinosaurs had to live in warm climates or be able to burrow underground in cold seasons. It also means that they would slow down and become inactive if their surroundings cooled much either at night or at other times. And they would have to bask in the sun in order to get going again, to move and seek food. And finally, if dinosaurs were ectotherms, they would have spent most of their lives resting or moving slowly. Like the lizards of today, they could make some quick moves for a little while, but would tire easily.

Perhaps this is why Richard Owen imagined that Iguanodon was built somewhat like a lumbering rhinoceros. It certainly explains why many paleontologists called a big dinosaur such as Brontosaurus "sluggish." Marsh called it a "stupid, slow-moving reptile." This dinosaur and other sauropods were usually thought to be lake-dwellers—perhaps needing the buoyancy of water to support their great bulk.

Some early paleontologists wondered about these widely accepted ideas. Edward Cope toyed with the idea that sauropods lived on land and looked something like giraffes. Their long necks would enable them to reach high into treetops for leaves to eat. But Cope put aside this idea.

Even though there were bulky dinosaurs such as Brontosaurus and squat, tank-like ones such as Triceratops, fossil-collectors discovered many others that were far from sluggish in form. There were the ostrich dinosaurs with their long hind legs, well suited for fast running. It is easy to picture them zooming along at fifty miles per hour. But an ectothermic reptile would tire quickly if it tried to move that fast.

There was also *Saurornithoides* ("bird-like reptile") found in Mongolia in 1922. This slender dinosaur had grasping "hands," a large brain, and big eyes, as birds do. It definitely did not seem like a "stupid, slow-moving" animal.

In museum exhibits some dinosaurs are shown in running poses. Paleontologists have also approved drawings that show highly active dinosaurs. Still, the idea that dinosaurs were ectothermic reptiles lived on, partly because scientists did not fully understand some of the differences between ectotherms and endotherms.

One difference lies simply in the way the animals stand. The legs of living reptiles sprawl out to the sides of their bodies. Some drawings by early paleontologists showed dinosaurs' legs that way too. However, the shoulder sockets of most dinosaurs face down, not out. Their leg bones fit directly under the weight of their bodies. This means that dinosaurs stood upright. They did not sprawl and crawl as lizards do. The skeletons of

For many years sauropods like Diplodocus were thought to be squat, sluggish dwellers of lakes and marshes.

Brontosaurus and other sauropods are similar to elephants and other mammals that stand on all four legs. The skeletons of Iguanodon, Tyrannosaurus, Saurornithoides, and many others are similar to those of birds.

Among today's living animals, only endotherms—birds and mammals—stand upright. This suggests, but does not prove, that dinosaurs were endotherms. Also, an

| Camarasaurus | Barosaurus | Apatosaurus (Brontosaurus) |

A modern view of sauropods shows them on dry land, standing erect like elephants and browsing on evergreens.

animal that stands upright usually has its head and brain well above its heart. In the case of some sauropod dinosaurs, blood had to be pumped upward as much as 18 feet from heart to head. This suggests that some dinosaurs had powerful, well-developed hearts like today's endotherms, not like today's reptiles.

These differences, and their importance, were recognized only in recent years. In the 1960s, several paleontologists had nagging doubts about whether dinosaurs had been "cold-blooded" ectotherms. One of these scientists was John Ostrom, of the Peabody Museum of Natural History at Yale University. He already had a reputation for challenging long-accepted ideas about dinosaurs. Ostrom had re-examined fossils of duck-billed dinosaurs and had shown that these animals lived mostly on land, not in lakes and marshes, as had been believed.

In 1964, Ostrom discovered an unusual dinosaur in Montana. Called *Deinonychus,* this eight-foot-long animal had sharp teeth and slender but strong front legs, tipped with claws. On each hind foot were two normal claws and one bigger, sickle-shaped claw. Judging from its appearance, Ostrom concluded that this claw was always held off the ground. It had some use other than walking.

John Ostrom believes that this dinosaur killed others with its special hind claws. As the prey of Deinonychus struggled to get away or fight back, this dinosaur held on with its long, grasping front legs. Then it hopped quickly from one hind foot to the other, making quick slashes with its big sickle claws.

In 1969, describing Deinonychus in a scientific journal, Ostrom wrote, "It must have been a fleet-footed ... extremely agile and very active animal."

That same year John Ostrom offered the world a new view of dinosaurs. They were a widely varied group, and some may have been ectotherms like today's reptiles. But many may have been endotherms, much more like today's birds and mammals. They may have been the dashing dinosaurs!

The extraordinary Deinonychus—
"fleet-footed . . . extremely agile . . .
very active."

6

A REVOLUTION BEGINS

Lively, energetic dinosaurs? The idea was sharply questioned by some scientists. And this matter is still not settled, simply because matters are never quite "settled" in science. They are always open to question, just as the image of sluggish dinosaurs was.

This revolutionary idea about dinosaurs is now accepted by some paleontologists but not all. Supporting evidence has been found by several scientists, including a French paleontologist, Armand de Ricqles of the University of Paris. He knew that fine details of once-living bones can often be observed in fossils. Regardless of a bone's age, study under a microscope can reveal a lot about the creature it came from. Professor de Ricqles used special equipment to make paper-thin cross-sections of bones. Some were from recently killed reptiles and mammals, some from dinosaurs.

He found that the bones of most lizards and other reptiles have few blood vessels. This is what you might expect from low-energy animals. The dinosaur bones were different. Every one examined had many blood vessels.

They were well suited for carrying plenty of food and oxygen to the dinosaur's cells. They were like mammal bones. They were like *our* bones.

So the bones of dinosaurs, objects that had been collected by the ton and studied and restudied for so many years, were investigated in a new way and provided more evidence that dinosaurs may have been endotherms.

Further proof came from the studies of Robert Bakker (pronounced Back-er), a young paleontologist who had worked with John Ostrom. Bakker is now a professor at Johns Hopkins University in Maryland. Like many other paleontologists, he became interested in ancient life at an early age. In fact, he remembers exactly when dinosaurs caught his interest.

"It was an article in *Life* that did it," he recalls. "In the fifties. With a fantastic foldout of all the dinosaurs.... I remember exactly where I was. At my grandfather's house. I sat there, and I got hooked."

After studying to become a paleontologist, Robert Bakker took some basic ideas about the lives of modern animals and checked to see whether they applied to dinosaurs. We know that predatory mammals (those that kill others for food) need a lot of food energy. Predators such as lions, wolves, and cheetahs eat their own weight in meat every few weeks or so.

In order to get enough food, such predators must live with large populations of prey. One example is the Serengeti Plain in Tanzania, Africa, where vast herds of grazing mammals are preyed upon by much smaller numbers of lions, cheetahs, hyenas, and other predators.

The situation is quite different with such ectotherms

as lizards and crocodiles. They use less energy than endotherms, so they need less food. Predatory reptiles do not need to live with large numbers of prey animals.

Bakker believed that these facts about the ecology of living animals could be applied to ancient ones. He spent many months studying fossils that had been collected from different times in earth history. In the Permian Period, a time of reptiles that lived *before* the dinosaurs, he found no great difference in the numbers of predators and prey. In the Cenozoic Era, *after* the time of dinosaurs, he found many more fossils of prey mammals than of predatory mammals.

What about the Mesozoic Era, when dinosaurs ruled the land? Bakker found that the numbers of predatory dinosaurs were few compared with those of their prey. There were, for example, many more plant-eating horned dinosaurs than meat-eaters like Tyrannosaurus. The ecology of dinosaur communities was similar to that of the mammals that lived later in the Cenozoic Era and that live in Africa today. According to Bakker's studies of many fossil collections, dinosaurs had the ecology of endotherms.

Some scientists wonder whether such conclusions can be drawn from fossil collections. Can we really reconstruct a 100-million-year-old dinosaur community with any accuracy? Perhaps some kinds of dinosaurs behaved in ways that kept them from dying in places where their bones would be likely to become fossils. Perhaps plant-eating dinosaurs were more likely to become fossilized.

Robert Bakker and other paleontologists have considered these questions. There *are* places where certain kinds of dinosaurs were fossilized and others were not. Many skeletons of predators have been found in one area of Utah. Perhaps a few were trapped in mud, tar, or quicksand. Then other predators, looking for an easy meal, became trapped too.

There are many mysteries about how and why animals are preserved as fossils. Overall, however, the world-wide evidence from fossils suggests a picture of dinosaur life similar to that of animal life on the Serengeti Plain today—vast mixed herds of plant-eating dinosaurs being stalked and chased by packs of predatory dinosaurs.

Once we begin to think of dinosaurs as endotherms, some old puzzles may be solved, but some new ones are created. For example, people have often wondered why mammals were so insignificant for most of their history. They have been around for 200 million years. Yet only during the past 65 million years have they flourished. Today, they are the most abundant and successful large and medium-sized animals on land. We live in, and are part of, the Age of Mammals. In contrast, reptiles are rather insignificant today. As ectotherms, they do not compete well with mammals and birds.

In light of this, what was the Mesozoic Era really like? Were sluggish dinosaurs competing with energetic, lively mammals—and winning? That seems unlikely. Some paleontologists believe that the only way dinosaurs could "beat" the mammals was to be highly energetic themselves. The smaller dinosaurs probably tried to eat the little mammals, which survived by being able to hide in small places and perhaps by being active at night. Today's Age of Mammals became possible only when one

Evidence from fossil collections shows that packs of meat-eating dinosaurs preyed on herds of plant-eaters. Gorgosaurids feed on a Stegosaurus *(left);* a Saurornithoides chases down a Parkosaurus *(below).*

group of endotherms—the dinosaurs—disappeared as large land animals and allowed the mammals to flourish.

The question *why* the hugely successful dinosaurs died out remains unanswered and controversial. The cause (or causes) affected not just dinosaurs but also some plants on land and plankton in the seas. Some people believe that a change in climate—perhaps a rapid cooling—caused this extraordinary mass extinction.

Knowing that dinosaurs may have been endotherms helps clear up some puzzles about the earth's past climate. Until recently, if scientists found dinosaur fossils in certain layers of rocks in a certain area, they assumed that the climate there had been a warm, tropical one. Otherwise the "cold blooded" dinosaurs could not have lived there. In 1969 John Ostrom pointed out that dinosaurs could no longer be used as clues to warm climates. If they were endotherms, dinosaurs could live in a variety of climates, just as mammals and birds do today.

If dinosaurs lived in areas with cold nights and cold seasons, they may have needed insulation to conserve their body heat. Birds are insulated by feathers, and many mammals by hair. Perhaps some dinosaurs were insulated by layers of fat, overlapping scales, or even by feathers. Soft parts like flesh, feathers, and skin rarely become fossils, so we may never know much about dinosaur insulation.

Dinosaurs in warm climates would not need insulation, just as today's elephants and rhinos do not. However, endotherms in warm climates and seasons sometimes have the problem of needing to lose body heat.

Dogs pant to let out heat, and many other mammals lose heat by sweating. Dinosaurs, too, may have had ways to lose heat from their bodies. According to James Farlow, a paleontologist at Yale University, this was the function of the peculiar plates on the back of Stegosaurus.

This dinosaur has stimulated controversy ever since it was discovered in 1877. Its name means "plated lizard," and the plates caused plenty of scientific debate about their use and arrangement. Eventually it was agreed that the plates were in two rows on the dinosaur's back, and they alternated, one on the left, one on the right, and so on.

It was widely believed that the plates were armor that protected Stegosaurus from predators. James Farlow had another explanation. In 1976 he proposed that the plates helped rid Stegosaurus of excess body heat. X-rays and other close examination of the plates revealed that they were not solid bone but had a network of spaces for blood vessels. They probably received a rich flow of blood whenever a Stegosaurus needed to lose heat. Engineers tested the shapes and arrangement of the plates in wind tunnels. They found that the plates were ideally suited for exposing a large surface area to the air, which would then carry away heat from the plates. Farlow concluded that the plates were cooling devices. They would have been very useful for an overheated—and perhaps endo-thermic—Stegosaurus on hot summer days.

This came as surprising news to people who grew up reading about the "armor" plates of Stegosaurus. Of course the plates may have cooled *and* protected Stegosaurus.

All sorts of old notions about dinosaurs are tumbling down. Perhaps the most startling idea, so far, was suggested by John Ostrom in 1973. He offered evidence that birds evolved from dinosaurs. The skeletons of some small dinosaurs are almost identical to *Archeopteryx,* the famous first-known bird. But why use the term "bird" at all? Instead, Archeopteryx can be thought of as a feathered dinosaur and birds as the dinosaur group that lived on after other kinds died out.

This led to yet another startling idea, advocated by Robert Bakker. For centuries, birds have been classified in a group called Aves, and dinosaurs in Reptilia. Bakker proposes that this classification be changed. Class Dinosauria would be created and Class Aves eliminated. Since birds are "living expressions of basic dinosaur biology," they would be classified as a sub-group of dinosaurs.

It is fun to think of the possibilities in this proposal.

Stegosaurus was once believed to have plates all over its back; now the arrangement shown at the right is thought to have helped cool the dinosaur.

Imagine, in wintertime, putting seeds in your dinosaur feeder, and, in spring, watching and listening for the return of the beautiful spring dinosaurs! But we don't yet have to give up the term "bird." Remember, Richard Owen made the name dinosaur from Greek words meaning "terrible lizard." Terrible or not, dinosaurs were not lizards. Instead of Dinosauria, perhaps the dinosaurs and their descendants, the birds, deserve an entirely new and more accurate name for their class.

A revolution in ideas about dinosaurs is underway. It will have many effects, great and small. People may even change their feelings about dinosaurs. Many people are repelled by living reptiles, and this has probably influenced their feelings toward dinosaurs. It has helped dinosaurs seem "creepy" and scary. Artists have painted dinosaurs to look this way.

Now we have reason to believe that some dinosaurs were endotherms. They were much more like birds and mammals than reptiles. Perhaps some small dinosaurs were rather cute and cuddly. Perhaps some of the bigger ones were as graceful and beautiful and likable as horses or deer.

We may never know. But we can be sure that the story of dinosaurs and people is on the threshold of a wonderful new era of investigation and discovery.

FURTHER READING

Bakker, Robert T. "Dinosaur Renaissance." *Scientific American,* April 1975, pp. 58-78.

Colbert, Edwin H. *Men and Dinosaurs.* New York: E. P. Dutton, 1968.

De Camp, L. Sprague and Catherine. *The Day of the Dinosaur.* New York: Doubleday, 1968.

Desmond, Adrian. "Central Park's Fragile Dinosaurs." *Natural History,* October 1974, pp. 65-71.

————. *The Hot-Blooded Dinosaurs.* New York: Dial Press, 1976.

Farlow, James O., *et al.* "Plates of Dinosaur Stegosaurus: Forced Convection Heat Loss Fins?" *Science,* June 11, 1976, pp. 1123-1125.

Gould, Stephen Jay. "The Telltale Wishbone." *Natural History,* November 1977, pp. 26-34.

————. "Were Dinosaurs Dumb?" *Natural History,* May 1978, pp. 9-12, 16.

Ipsen, D. C. *The Riddle of the Stegosaurus.* Reading, Mass.: Addison-Wesley, 1969.

Kielan-Jaworowska, Zofia. *Hunting for Dinosaurs.* Cambridge, Mass.: MIT Press, 1969.

Marx, Jean. "Warm-Blooded Dinosaurs: Evidence Pro and Con." *Science,* March 31, 1978, pp. 1424-1426.

Ostrom, John. "Terrible Claw" (Deinonychus). *Discovery,* Fall 1969, pp. 1-9.

INDEX

Numbers in boldface refer to illustrations.

63